Write In

Happy

Journal

Write In *Happy* Journal

Write In Books –

Blank Books You Can Write In

Featuring:

160 Pages devoted to Journaling

60 Pages devoted to Memorable Moments

Each journal line has an extra section which can be used for dates and/or numbering

Copyright © 2014 by H Barnett

All rights reserved.

Write In Happy Journal

CONTENTS

JOURNAL 5

MEMORABLE MOMENTS 157

Write In Happy Journal

Follow your heart; dream big and above all –

Appreciate how amazing life is!

Write In *Happy* Journal

JOURNAL

Write In *Happy* Journal

JOURNAL

Write In *Happy* Journal

JOURNAL

Write In *Happy* Journal

JOURNAL

Write In *Happy* Journal

JOURNAL

Write In *Happy* Journal

JOURNAL

Write In *Happy* Journal

JOURNAL

Write In *Happy* Journal

JOURNAL

Write In *Happy* Journal

JOURNAL

Write In *Happy* Journal

JOURNAL

Write In *Happy* Journal

JOURNAL

Write In *Happy* Journal

JOURNAL

Write In *Happy* Journal

JOURNAL

Write In Happy Journal

JOURNAL

Write In *Happy* Journal

JOURNAL

Write In *Happy* Journal

JOURNAL

Write In *Happy* Journal

JOURNAL

Write In *Happy* Journal

JOURNAL

Write In *Happy* Journal

JOURNAL

Write In *Happy* Journal

JOURNAL

Write In *Happy* Journal

JOURNAL

Write In *Happy* Journal

JOURNAL

Write In *Happy* Journal

JOURNAL

Write In *Happy* Journal

JOURNAL

Write In *Happy* Journal

JOURNAL

Write In *Happy* Journal

JOURNAL

Write In *Happy* Journal

JOURNAL

Write In *Happy* Journal

JOURNAL

Write In *Happy* Journal

JOURNAL

Write In *Happy* Journal

JOURNAL

Write In *Happy* Journal

JOURNAL

Write In *Happy* Journal

JOURNAL

Write In *Happy* Journal

JOURNAL

Write In *Happy* Journal

JOURNAL

Write In *Happy* Journal

JOURNAL

Write In *Happy* Journal

JOURNAL

Write In *Happy* Journal

JOURNAL

Write In *Happy* Journal

JOURNAL

Write In *Happy* Journal

JOURNAL

Write In *Happy* Journal

JOURNAL

Write In *Happy* Journal

JOURNAL

Write In *Happy* Journal

JOURNAL

Write In *Happy* Journal

JOURNAL

Write In *Happy* Journal

JOURNAL

Write In *Happy* Journal

JOURNAL

Write In *Happy* Journal

JOURNAL

Write In *Happy* Journal

JOURNAL

Write In *Happy* Journal

JOURNAL

Write In *Happy* Journal

JOURNAL

Write In *Happy* Journal

JOURNAL

Write In *Happy* Journal

JOURNAL

Write In *Happy* Journal

JOURNAL

Write In Happy Journal

JOURNAL

Write In *Happy* Journal

JOURNAL

Write In *Happy* Journal

JOURNAL

Write In *Happy* Journal

JOURNAL

Write In *Happy* Journal

JOURNAL

Write In Happy Journal

JOURNAL

Write In *Happy* Journal

JOURNAL

Write In *Happy* Journal

JOURNAL

Write In Happy Journal

JOURNAL

Write In *Happy* Journal

JOURNAL

Write In *Happy* Journal

JOURNAL

Write In *Happy* Journal

JOURNAL

Write In *Happy* Journal

JOURNAL

Write In *Happy* Journal

JOURNAL

Write In *Happy* Journal

JOURNAL

Write In *Happy* Journal

JOURNAL

Write In Happy Journal

JOURNAL

Write In *Happy* Journal

JOURNAL

Write In *Happy* Journal

JOURNAL

Write In *Happy* Journal

JOURNAL

Write In *Happy* Journal

JOURNAL

Write In *Happy* Journal

JOURNAL

Write In *Happy* Journal

JOURNAL

Write In *Happy* Journal

JOURNAL

Write In *Happy* Journal

JOURNAL

Write In *Happy* Journal

JOURNAL

Write In *Happy* Journal

JOURNAL

Write In *Happy* Journal

JOURNAL

Write In *Happy* Journal

JOURNAL

Write In *Happy* Journal

JOURNAL

Write In *Happy* Journal

JOURNAL

Write In *Happy* Journal

JOURNAL

Write In *Happy* Journal

JOURNAL

Write In *Happy* Journal

JOURNAL

Write In *Happy* Journal

JOURNAL

Write In Happy Journal

JOURNAL

Write In *Happy* Journal

JOURNAL

Write In Happy Journal

JOURNAL

Write In *Happy* Journal

JOURNAL

Write In Happy Journal

JOURNAL

Write In *Happy* Journal

JOURNAL

Write In *Happy* Journal

JOURNAL

Write In *Happy* Journal

JOURNAL

Write In *Happy* Journal

JOURNAL

Write In *Happy* Journal

JOURNAL

Write In Happy Journal

JOURNAL

Write In *Happy* Journal

JOURNAL

Write In *Happy* Journal

JOURNAL

Write In *Happy* Journal

JOURNAL

Write In *Happy* Journal

JOURNAL

Write In *Happy* Journal

JOURNAL

Write In Happy Journal

JOURNAL

Write In *Happy* **Journal**

JOURNAL

Write In Happy Journal

JOURNAL

Write In *Happy* Journal

JOURNAL

Write In *Happy* Journal

JOURNAL

Write In *Happy* Journal

JOURNAL

Write In *Happy* Journal

JOURNAL

Write In *Happy* Journal

JOURNAL

Write In *Happy* Journal

JOURNAL

Write In *Happy* Journal

JOURNAL

Write In *Happy* Journal

JOURNAL

Write In *Happy* Journal

JOURNAL

Write In *Happy* Journal

JOURNAL

Write In *Happy* Journal

JOURNAL

Write In *Happy* Journal

JOURNAL

Write In *Happy* Journal

JOURNAL

Write In *Happy* Journal

JOURNAL

Write In *Happy* Journal

JOURNAL

Write In *Happy* Journal

JOURNAL

Write In Happy Journal

JOURNAL

Write In *Happy* Journal

JOURNAL

Write In *Happy* Journal

JOURNAL

Write In *Happy* Journal

JOURNAL

Write In *Happy* Journal

JOURNAL

Write In *Happy* Journal

JOURNAL

Write In *Happy* Journal

JOURNAL

Write In *Happy* Journal

JOURNAL

Write In *Happy* Journal

JOURNAL

Write In *Happy* Journal

JOURNAL

Write In *Happy* Journal

JOURNAL

Write In *Happy* Journal

JOURNAL

Write In *Happy* Journal

JOURNAL

Write In Happy Journal

JOURNAL

Write In *Happy* Journal

JOURNAL

Write In *Happy* Journal

JOURNAL

Write In *Happy* Journal

JOURNAL

Write In Happy Journal

JOURNAL

Write In *Happy* Journal

JOURNAL

Write In Happy Journal

JOURNAL

Write In *Happy* **Journal**

JOURNAL

Write In *Happy* Journal

JOURNAL

Write In *Happy* Journal

JOURNAL

Write In *Happy* Journal

JOURNAL

Write In *Happy* Journal

JOURNAL

Write In *Happy* Journal

JOURNAL

Write In *Happy* Journal

JOURNAL

Write In *Happy* Journal

JOURNAL

Write In *Happy* Journal

JOURNAL

Write In *Happy* Journal

JOURNAL

Write In *Happy* Journal

MEMORABLE MOMENTS

Write In *Happy* Journal

MEMORABLE MOMENTS

Draw doodles, write quotes, or quick notes.

Write In *Happy* Journal

MEMORABLE MOMENTS

Write In *Happy* Journal

MEMORABLE MOMENTS

Draw doodles, write quotes, or quick notes.

Write In *Happy* Journal

MEMORABLE MOMENTS

Write In *Happy* Journal

MEMORABLE MOMENTS

Draw doodles, write quotes, or quick notes.

Write In *Happy* Journal

MEMORABLE MOMENTS

Write In Happy Journal

MEMORABLE MOMENTS

Draw doodles, write quotes, or quick notes.

Write In *Happy* Journal

MEMORABLE MOMENTS

Write In *Happy* Journal

MEMORABLE MOMENTS

Draw doodles, write quotes, or quick notes.

Write In *Happy* Journal

MEMORABLE MOMENTS

Write In *Happy* Journal

MEMORABLE MOMENTS

Draw doodles, write quotes, or quick notes.

Write In *Happy* Journal

MEMORABLE MOMENTS

Write In *Happy* Journal

MEMORABLE MOMENTS

Draw doodles, write quotes, or quick notes.

Write In *Happy* Journal

MEMORABLE MOMENTS

Write In *Happy* Journal

MEMORABLE MOMENTS

Draw doodles, write quotes, or quick notes.

Write In *Happy* Journal

MEMORABLE MOMENTS

Write In *Happy* Journal

MEMORABLE MOMENTS

Draw doodles, write quotes, or quick notes.

Write In *Happy* Journal

MEMORABLE MOMENTS

Write In *Happy* Journal

MEMORABLE MOMENTS

Draw doodles, write quotes, or quick notes.

Write In *Happy* Journal

MEMORABLE MOMENTS

Write In *Happy* Journal

MEMORABLE MOMENTS

Draw doodles, write quotes, or quick notes.

Write In *Happy* Journal

MEMORABLE MOMENTS

Write In *Happy* Journal

MEMORABLE MOMENTS

Draw doodles, write quotes, or quick notes.

Write In *Happy* Journal

MEMORABLE MOMENTS

Write In *Happy* Journal

MEMORABLE MOMENTS

Draw doodles, write quotes, or quick notes.

Write In *Happy* Journal

MEMORABLE MOMENTS

Write In *Happy* Journal

MEMORABLE MOMENTS

Draw doodles, write quotes, or quick notes.

Write In *Happy* Journal

MEMORABLE MOMENTS

Write In *Happy* Journal

MEMORABLE MOMENTS

Draw doodles, write quotes, or quick notes.

Write In *Happy* Journal

MEMORABLE MOMENTS

Write In *Happy* Journal

MEMORABLE MOMENTS

Draw doodles, write quotes, or quick notes.

Write In *Happy* Journal

MEMORABLE MOMENTS

Write In Happy Journal

MEMORABLE MOMENTS

Draw doodles, write quotes, or quick notes.

Write In Happy Journal

MEMORABLE MOMENTS

Write In *Happy* Journal

MEMORABLE MOMENTS

Draw doodles, write quotes, or quick notes.

Write In *Happy* Journal

MEMORABLE MOMENTS

Write In *Happy* Journal

MEMORABLE MOMENTS

Draw doodles, write quotes, or quick notes.

Write In *Happy* Journal

MEMORABLE MOMENTS

Write In *Happy* Journal

MEMORABLE MOMENTS

Draw doodles, write quotes, or quick notes.

Write In *Happy* Journal

MEMORABLE MOMENTS

Write In *Happy* Journal

MEMORABLE MOMENTS

Draw doodles, write quotes, or quick notes.

Write In *Happy* Journal

MEMORABLE MOMENTS

Write In *Happy* Journal

MEMORABLE MOMENTS

Draw doodles, write quotes, or quick notes.

Write In *Happy* Journal

MEMORABLE MOMENTS

Write In *Happy* Journal

MEMORABLE MOMENTS

Draw doodles, write quotes, or quick notes.

Write In *Happy* Journal

MEMORABLE MOMENTS

Write In *Happy* Journal

MEMORABLE MOMENTS

Draw doodles, write quotes, or quick notes.

Write In *Happy* Journal

MEMORABLE MOMENTS

Write In *Happy* Journal

MEMORABLE MOMENTS

Draw doodles, write quotes, or quick notes.

Write In *Happy* Journal

MEMORABLE MOMENTS

Write In *Happy* Journal

MEMORABLE MOMENTS

Draw doodles, write quotes, or quick notes.

Write In *Happy* Journal

MEMORABLE MOMENTS

Write In *Happy* Journal

MEMORABLE MOMENTS

Draw doodles, write quotes, or quick notes.

Write In *Happy* Journal

MEMORABLE MOMENTS

Write In *Happy* Journal

MEMORABLE MOMENTS

Draw doodles, write quotes, or quick notes.

Write In *Happy* Journal

MEMORABLE MOMENTS

Write In *Happy* Journal

MEMORABLE MOMENTS

Draw doodles, write quotes, or quick notes.

Write In *Happy* Journal

MEMORABLE MOMENTS

Write In *Happy* Journal

MEMORABLE MOMENTS

Draw doodles, write quotes, or quick notes.

Write In *Happy* Journal

MEMORABLE MOMENTS

Write In Happy Journal

MEMORABLE MOMENTS

Draw doodles, write quotes, or quick notes.

Write In *Happy* Journal

MEMORABLE MOMENTS

Write In Happy Journal

If you have a positive heart, you'll know how to encourage others.

If you feel grateful inside, you'll know how to appreciate, not only yourself, but others as well.

If you like and love yourself, you'll also discover love in the people around you.

Thank you for being so wonderful!

Made in the USA
San Bernardino, CA
25 November 2014